LOVING

Heather Goddin

HEATHER GODDIN

LOVING

Matador
9 Priory Business Park,
Wistow Road, Kibworth Beauchamp,
Leicestershire. LE8 0RX
Tel: 0116 279 2299
Email: books@troubador.co.uk
Web: www.troubador.co.uk/matador
Twitter: @matadorbooks

ISBN 978 1789013 818
British Library Cataloguing in Publication Data.
A catalogue record for this book is available from the British Library.

Printed and bound by CPI Group (UK) Ltd, Croydon, CR0 4YY
Typeset in 11pt Minion Pro by Troubador Publishing Ltd, Leicester, UK

Matador is an imprint of Troubador Publishing Ltd

For Christer
Who loves life
as much as I do

LOVING

When I am with you
I am so filled with happiness
I feel like fizz in a bottle
And should it blow the cork
Then, heaven knows
What happens next.

When your hand touches mine
And I see the short gold hairs upon your wrist,
I think of your fingers' gentle strength
And my heart turns somersaults
Quite out of control.

When we talk to one another
And you smile at me
My bones dissolve
And I am turned quite inside out
With joy that feels like pain.

As time draws near when we must part,
When you lean your head on mine,
When we embrace
And our smiles cling to one another,
You do not know I bleed inside
At thought of leaving you.

2010

LAUGHARNE
(HOME OF DYLAN THOMAS)

This is the place he loved,
That drunken poet
Who plucked music from the air
And turned it into words.

I crossed the stream in spate
And took the path beneath the ruined castle wall
Towards the boathouse where he worked
And drank, undoubtedly, as well.

The river here is wide,
The ebb-tide shallows silvered by the sun.
The golden sands stretch out towards the open sea.

Clouds scudded overhead and blotted out the sun,
Tarnishing shallows and darkening the sands.
I sat and listened to the silence
Pierced only by the cry of birds.
Oyster-catcher, curlew and the seamew gull.
Whilst far away across the sand
A flight of plovers rose against the sky.
I watched the play of light
Across the low green hills.

There was another soul to share the peace.
An old man with a small, black grizzled dog.
By mutual consent we did no more than smile
And pass the time of day.
I saw the sadness in his face
Yet I did not speak and nor did he
But his old dog came and paid me his respects
Before I walked away.

2013

HARE

Through the glass door of my kitchen,
That opens into the garden,
I catch a movement from the corner of my eye.
A rabbit, perhaps?

But no, there on my step, peering in
A leveret, too young to yet know fear.
Confused, out of his depth, perhaps.
We gazed at one another
Through the glass.

I am entranced, so close are we.
I see the pinkness in each ear
And on his nose.
The great brown eyes.

What do I do?
If I open the door he might get in
(How do you catch a hare inside a house?)
But no, he lollops off
And disappears from sight.

Only this morning, early, as I made my tea,
Two young partridges stood on that step
Tapping their beaks upon the glass.
What next I wonder?

2017

LEMMINGS

I have come to the conclusion
That you are a lemming.
Set on running to that cliff
For the suicidal jump,
Ignoring all hazards on the way.
Whilst I have to watch you do it,
Never lifting a finger to stop you
For this is what you want.

I think I am a lemming, too
But travelling at a slower rate.
Limping along behind the throng.
Intent on lurching to the brink.

But our reasons are different.
Your journey is for love of God.
Mine for love of you.
You may survive the fall.
Carry on swimming for a while.
My end will be kinder
For I never learnt to swim.

2012

DAYBREAK

I lie beside you in the summer dawn.
Lying awake, afraid to miss one single hour of you,
Watching you sleep.
Storing up memories for a rainy day.

In the field by the river
The fox barks twice.
After the midnight heat
The air strikes chill.
I want to creep close to you
But I do not want to break your quiet sleep,
Loving these secret moments of your privacy.

High in the branches of the tree beside the house,
The blackbird starts his big, deep-throated song,
Laced with the pain of doubts and fears and loss.

Soft-fingered dawn lights up the corners of the blind.
Your sleeping face is calm. Shut off from me.
Blackbird and thrush mingle their songs
In mindless ecstasy.
The sunlight promises another lovely day.

At last, you stir and wake,
Turning towards me in the bed.
Your eyes smile greeting.
We are no longer two but one.
And your body's message
Melts away fear in birdsong and light.

1985

PHEASANTS

How can something so beautiful be so gormless?
A brain the size of a pea
Crammed with panic and confusion,
Changing its mind in the middle of the road
As to which route to take.
Stuck in the path of lorries and cars
With a runway too short to take off.
Sometimes one tries a "Kamikaze" end.
Targeting a windscreen, shattering glass,
Making a nasty mess on the road.
Not even fit to eat.

Today one stood on a roof across the lane,
Loudly proclaiming in that dreadful voice
(Creaking gate in need of oil?)
"I am the king of the castle."
And then comes doubt.
"But how did I get here
And how do I get off?"
Teetering on the edge and dithering,
He managed to get off.
But more like a sack of potatoes
Than a bird.

Just now he stands upon the garden wall
In his courtship coat.
So beautiful and yet so dumb.

2012

TECHNOLOGY

I drown in a sea of technology.
Surrounded by alien words.
A language I've not learnt.
Google and Twitter. Ipad and Wii.
Surfing the net and trawling the web.

To me, a web is something spiders weave,
A mouse a tiny creature,
Four legs, bright eyes, a tail,
(Something rude in Swedish.)
Online is how you catch a fish.
Surfing is a seaside sport.

I do not want the Internet.
Addictive, filled with danger,
Discriminates between the ones who "have"
And simple souls who don't.

I'd keep the mobile for emergencies
(A plague on e-mails and all texts.)
There is no happier sound than a loved one's voice
Upon the telephone.
No better sight than writing on an envelope
Sitting on the mat.

2008

MOUNTAIN

I've always loved the mountains
But not to climb.
I look at them in all their moods
With wonder and with awe.
Preferably at a distance.

Even from a distance they hold their power.
Alluring, mysterious they call to me.
Bastions of rock. Dwarfing the sky
But when I reach the foothills my courage fails.
They are too big, too vast, too high.

Then why do I climb this mountain?
Is my name Mahomet?
No, it is not.
Two steps forward, one step back
On a slippery slope.
Sometimes the route is easy and my heart is light
But often the way is blocked by rocks
Or the mists blot out the path
And I plod on in bleak despair.

Whether I reach the summit remains to be seen.
So why do I still climb this mountain?
If I want to reach my goal
I really have no choice.

What have I begun?

2007

WILD LILACS

They perfume the air with their sweetness
And with their beauty gladden the eye.
From deepest purple shading down through lilac and mauve
To purest bridal white.

Once a house stood here, long since gone.
The garden plot is now a wilderness
With rampant grass and meadow flowers.
I wonder who they were,
The ones who planted the lilac trees
For the springtime glory of the garden?
Living or dead, wherever they may be,
As long as the old trees live
Something of them lingers on.

2008

At the New Year

I stand at the edge of the year
Watching the past fall away.

Something is happening
Not yet explained or fully understood,
From which there can be now no turning back.
Unsure of the future yet ready to go.
For good or ill
My life will never be the same again.

The winds of change are blowing through my life,
Opening doors I never knew were there.
I can see brightness in the sky
Beyond the windows of my mind.
The darkest clouds have rolled away.
It promises a glorious day.

2007/2008

JOURNEY

My heart sleeps,
Numb with the pain of leaving you,
On the empty roads between the forests of pine and birch
And the placid silver lakes
Under a cloudy sky.

My heart begins to stir
In the secret valleys clad with trees
Along the deep, blue rivers
And the towering hills
Under an even bluer sky.

My heart begins to sing a sad lament
High on the roof of the world.
Amongst the snows and frozen lakes,
The ice-blue rivers and the waterfalls
Rushing in spate to reach
The fjords below.

My heart is telling me
What I already know.
That time is short
And even in so brief a time
I am aware
That I would rather have six months with you
Than twenty years without.

2008

LONG DISTANCE CALL

I dial your number.
Listen to it ring,
Bridging the miles and the years
And I think of you lifting the phone
To answer my call.

At the sound of your voice
Joy surges through me,
Washing away the layers of time,
Flooding my senses,
Drowning me dumb.

In those earth-stopping seconds,
The splintering silence,
Can you not sense my love and my longing?
Or do you just think,
"Another wrong number?"
Before I ring off.

1997

DRAWBRIDGE

Sometimes, when things have gone swimmingly,
You suddenly raise the drawbridge.
I have probably come too close. Crossed the line
Or you see the heart worn so imprudently
On my sleeve.

So there I am, left halfway across the moat,
Hurt and frustrated, forced to retreat.
That is when I want to storm the castle.
Hurl my missiles onto the battlements
And mine the foundations.

But reason and common sense win the battle.
The only way ahead is to be calm.
So, I sit beside the moat and wait
For you to lower the drawbridge
And welcome me in.

2012/Revised 2014

Fools' Gold

Don't envy me, my friend,
For I am neither fish nor fowl.
You are in love with a mad idea,
Craving excitement in your life.
Romantic notions of a stolen love.

Reality is otherwise.
It is hunger and thirst,
A cold hearth and an empty cradle.
For me, the trap was sprung
Before I was aware of it.

Not for you, Fools' Gold,
Promising much and offering nothing.
You would never stand for it.
Your patience would run out.
Don't envy me, my friend.

1984

SEASONS

The seasons that you gave to me
Were Winter and Fall
But, often in the early days
The Summer blazed across the autumn leaves
And on bright days of winter sun,
Sheltered from wind and out of the shade,
The warmth still lingered on.
Yet I grudged the years before we met
For I never knew your Spring.

Now as I warm your wintry hands in mine,
You raise your head and smile.
Your eyes as bright as sun on April rain
And in their depths I see the ghost of Spring.
The Spring we never shared.

1999

VIGIL

We sit, the house and I, and wait,
Listening in the darkness and the silence.
The house has its secrets.
So have I.

Bells slash across the hot night air
As they have rung for centuries.
Chiming the quarters and the hours,
Calling the faithful to their prayers.
Cats fight and yowl in a nearby street.
The night wind sighs at the door.
The clock in the hall ticks endlessly on.

The house enfolds me,
Gathers me close in its silent serenity,
Sustaining life and nurturing hope.
We wait, the house and I.
It knows my secrets. Keeps its own.

1989

SUDDEN JOY

All that was wrong is suddenly right.
What was impossible now becomes simple.
That which was dark is instantly light.

I am a swallow, swirling and soaring,
Living-winged joy, scimitar sharp
In a burning blue sky.

I am a river, eternally singing
Through mountain and moorland
And midsummer fields.

I am the earth, sun-parched and barren,
Greedily drinking the life-giving waters
Of late-summer rain.

That which was dark is instantly light.
What was impossible now becomes easy.
All that was wrong is suddenly right.

2000

ABIGAIL

She bought one of my books from me
At a local craft fair in the town.
Young and intelligent. Different.
I liked her on sight
And when I came to sign her book
I asked her name.

"It's Abigail," she said,
"My mother saw it written on a mug
When I was on the way."

"Good choice," I said,
"It is a lovely name."

2017

IDIOMS, SAYINGS, QUOTATIONS

I won't beat about the bush,
Didn't you know it is dangerous
To wake a sleeping tiger?
But you set the cat among the pigeons
And *this* lion won't lie down with the lamb.

Wearing my heart on my sleeve
Has given you a stick to beat me with.
But sticks and stones can break my bones.
Cruel words cannot.
Hit back? Two wrongs will never make a right.
I'll turn the other cheek.

Old dogs can't learn to do new tricks.
The leopard can't change his spots.
I will tilt at windmills, chase the rainbows,
Cry for the moon.
For he who waits long at the ferry
Will one day get across.

It's no use crying over spilt milk.
One cannot make an omelette
Without breaking eggs.
What can't be cured must be endured.
Rain falls on the just and the unjust alike
But every cloud has a silver lining.

I am between a rock and a hard place
But I will not cut off my nose
To spite my face.
I must take my courage
In both hands.
Throw caution to the winds
And take the bull by the horns.
If the mountain won't come to Mahomet,
Mahomet must go to the mountain.

It is time to bury the hatchet.
Let bygones be bygones.
We have made a mountain out of a molehill.
It is a storm in a teacup.
Let us pour oil on troubled waters
For time and tide wait for no man.
Let us forgive and forget.

2013

THE SOCIAL LIFE OF MONKEYS

Watching a film about monkeys,
Their social life in the colony,
Their patterns of behaviour,
See them grooming each other.
I think how lucky they are
Just to belong.

You're always so elegant. Perfectly groomed.
Standing in front of you,
Queuing for something or other,
I feel you picking off hairs
From the back of my dress.
The parts I can't see.
Grooming me just like the monkeys.
Now I belong.

2017

SMILES

I have returned to this place, which I dreaded.
The place of landfalls and farewells.
My country of the heart.
This is your country, these are your people
In which I have no part.

I have scaled the walls of sorrow.
Walked the haunted paths of love
And on golden rocks beside a sapphire sea
I have shed the mask.
Facing your ghost
I can begin to heal.

In the shadowy bars where old men sit and drink
I am amongst your friends and mine.
I listen to them say, "He was the best."
Smiling, I nod, but do not say,
"He was the best, the very best and more."
Deep in the shadows I see the brilliance of your smile
And remember the first smiles that we gave one another.

2010

THOR'S HAMMER

Blood-red the sky at dawn,
Slate-grey silk the sea,
Shot with an angry crimson light.

At noon the wind began to blow,
The Viking wind, honed in the north,
Dragging the clouds across the sky,
Flattening the grasses of the shore,
Its breath as cold as ice.
Out in the bay, the sea began to rise,
Churning and roaring,
Spuming the rocks with icy foam.

Here, in the safety of the house,
I sit beside the fire
And listen to the battle of the wind and sea.
Above the tumult of the storm,
I seem to hear the shouts of fighting men,
The clamour of their arms.
Thor's Hammer pounding on the darkening shore.

The Norsemens' wind howls round the house,
Rattling at the windows, whistling at the door.
The house shakes at the onslaught
Of shrieking wind and driving rain.
I know no fear.
This house has stood two hundred years
And still will stand two hundred more.

But I wish that you were here with me,
Beside the dying fire,
To talk to me of flowers and summer seas
And hold my hand in yours.
But soon, quite soon, you will be home
And joy wells up to meet the storm.

1990

Negative and Positive

I fear the worst.
Ribbons of worry, tangled and twisted
Lie under my hand.
Panic strikes like the bite of a snake
Under the noon-day sun.
Fear stalks me in the night,
Soft-footed in the dark
And in the deepest caverns of my mind
The ice-cold terrors flow.

Cast out fear with love and faith.
Ribbons can be unravelled.
Snakes can be put to flight.
Face up to the beast in the dark.
Fill the caves with warmth and light
To melt the rivers of ice.

Think of the mountain snows.
Of tranquil seas and starry skies.
Look on the flowers, fair symbols of hope.
Fix on eternity, renewal of life.
Things may be better than they seem.

1994

SUITCASE OF DREAMS

I pack my suitcase for my trip,
Counting the days until we meet.
I take from my wardrobe
The clothes in which I know
I look my best.
For others have said,
Whose words mean nought to me,
"That looks good on you."
Vanity I know, but also the stuff of dreams.

For when we meet, what I want most
Is the warmth of your presence
And the smile upon your face,
When I hear you say,
"You look so elegant.
As always."

2010

Cocoa and Bedsocks

This is ridiculous at my age,
With my pension and bus pass,
When I should be thinking of cocoa and bedsocks
And remaking my will,
I go falling in love
And waiting for a letter with a foreign stamp.

I am as restless as a sapling in the wind,
Impatient as a cat upon the scrounge.
Moping like a lovesick girl.
Spinning my crazy dreams.
I know that he will write.
Unless I read the signals wrong?
Maybe he won't.

There was no post today,
Maybe I should settle for cocoa and bedsocks
But… tomorrow is another day.

2007

CANDLES

When the grey November dusk descends
Like a pall on the lifeless day,
I light my tiny candles
To cheer up my empty room.

They fill the darkness
With their gentle glow-worm light.
Bring to life
The smiling photos in their frames.
Awakening memories of happy days.
My silent guardians of the night.
Company of sorts.

They warm the deep, dark spaces of my room
And soothe my troubled heart.
My little crumbs of comfort.
My small, bright stars of hope.

2012

The Garden

I dreamt of a garden,
Beckoning from a distance,
Set between golden gates
Bathed in sunlight.
Stone-flagged paths all edged in box.
Bright beds of summer flowers.
The scent of roses in the air.
A peacock strutting on the lawn.
The garden framed by ancient oaks and conifers.

With happy heart I hurried on
Towards the shining place
But as I reached the golden gates
They clanged tight shut.
I could not find the catch.
I did not have a key.
And then I saw
They were not gold but black
But still I beat against the bars
Until my fingers bled.

And then I woke
Back in the cold, grey world again.

2010

MARGARET

When her husband died we did not understand
Her desperate display of grief
But once in a calm, quiet moment
She said to us,
"Nothing worse than this
Can ever happen to me now."
She had adored him
And sadly, none of us had ever really liked him.

Soon after, she began her own descent
Into a terminal illness,
Welcoming it like a friend.
But still she made a journey
To visit a place they'd always meant to go.
Well she did it
And then she died there,
Embracing death with something like joy.

Now, at last, I know how she felt
For when you came you gave me back my life
And if you die
You will take it away again.

Nothing worse could ever happen to me after that.

2017

HEATHERS

"What is your name?" she asked.
New neighbour in the village.
"Heather," I said,
"There're three of us along the street.
Heather, who lives next door to you,
Heather, who lives across the street from me
And then there's me, of course."

"No, four" she said,
"There's one who lives next door
To Richard and his wife,
Three houses down.
Old lady with a walking stick.
Writes poetry."

"That's me," I said.
"But she's got curly hair," she said,
"I noticed when I talked to her
Before we both moved in."

Desperate to prove a point,
I said, "*I'm* old.
When I stand up you'll see my walking stick.
My hair curls when there's dampness in the air
And I write poetry, as well."
She wasn't convinced.

How can I prove who I am?
My 'bus pass shows an egg with glasses.
My passport holds a grim, grey face
Of someone in the last sad days of terminal TB.
When I show them to my friends
They fall about laughing.

I give up.

2016

THE HIGH KING'S DAUGHTER

Oh, come with me to the mountain crags.
We will fly amongst the eagles and the buzzards
In the realms of highland deer
And the snow-white winter hare.
In the place of myrtle and heather
And wild, sweet mountain thyme.

Oh, come with me to the coral depths
Below the waves where the rainbow fishes swim,
Who will feed from our hands.
We will ride on the backs of whales
And lie amongst the friendly seals
On the golden beaches of the shore.

Oh come with me to the crystal caves
Of my father's hall, deep in the hills.
To dine with the Shining Ones, the *Daoine Sidhe*,
The ever-young, the beautiful
And feast from dishes of silver and gold
On faerie food, the food of dreams.

They say of us we have no hearts.
The *Daoine Sidhe*, the Lordly Ones,
The ever-young, the beautiful
But my mother was of mortal blood
And gave to me her human heart.
Stolen away from her mortal kin,
I watched her fade, grow old and die
Far from the world of men.

But I am the High King's daughter
And I know I must send you away, my dearest love,
Back to your mortal life.
For how could I bear to watch you pine,
Grow old and die in the human way
Whilst I live on alone.

You must go back to the world you know
Before you learn of the faerie ways.
To forget and find love with one of your kind.
Grow old and die in the way of all men.
Whilst I must live on in the way of immortals,
Never forgetting, doomed not to die.
What use then to me, my beauty, and my youth
When I long to be mortal with you.

2011

The Daoine Sidhe are from Celtic mythology. After the coming of Christianity,
they probably became angels or saints.

In Absence

I cannot hide what I feel.
I wear my heart upon my sleeve.
I cannot pretend to feel what I do not
And what you see is what I am.

I carry you with me
Through the restless patterns of my life
As I watch the seasons change.
I talk to you silently
Along the endless corridor of days
And will the time to pass…

You are my last thought before I sleep.
The first, so long before the dawn
And sometimes, in the night between,
I dream of you.

2011

BEBBUG

Walking across the square,
Someone would say to me,
"They've snails today at Joe's."
And I would join my friends
To feast on wine and snails.

The Maltese catch them in the fields
After the first life-giving rain of Autumn.
Take them home and starve them.
Put them in cages and feed them finest herbs
And succulent green plants,
Give them the time of their lives.

After a while they're sacrificed,
Cooked in garlic, wine and herbs.
How well I remember the taste.
We'd sit and gorge ourselves,
The shells piled high upon a plate.
Juices mopped up with crusty local bread,
Our meal washed down with rough red wine.

These are the days I don't forget.
The memories as fresh today
As when we sat and feasted in the sun.
So long ago and far away.

2017

Bebbug: a snail in Maltese.

LOST LOVE

I saw you in the street today,
Too far away to see your face,
Yet I knew you by the way you walked
And the way you held your head.

The road dividing us was wide
But still I would have run to you,
Forgetful of time and the passage of years,
Braving the traffic and the milling crowds,
To see your face light up at sight of me
And catch again your bright, remembered smile.

But time and distance held me back.
The fear that you would turn away from me.
And so, instead, I watched you slowly walk away
Out of my life again.

1999

BLOCKHUSUDDEN

There is a song by Rachmaninov
"How Fair This Place"
And when I come to Blockhusudden
It comes into my mind.
I share with it my happiness
And let it comfort me when I am low.
So close it is to the city
And yet it seems a million miles away.

In the café at the waterside
The sparrows come to share my meal,
Striving to reach, by devious means,
The crumbs upon my plate.
I watch the ocean liners, yachts and pleasure boats,
From my place beside the sea,
Sending their wash in noisy waves
To meet the shore beside my chair.

In summer it is busy.
The walkers and the joggers,
Equestrians and cyclists
Enjoying the woodland paths beside the sea.
But sometimes, out of season, there is no one here
And I can sit quietly and gaze out at some other isles
Stretching out to sea.
Peace and serenity. A place to unwind.
Birdsong in spring and summer
And always the sound of wind and sea.

I love this place.

2017

THE PATH THROUGH THE GLEN

I remember, so well, the path through the Glen
In early spring when snow still lay upon the mountain tops.
Snug in our oilskins and wellington boots,
We stomped and bounced on springy turf,
Splashing through puddles, relishing mud.
We searched for the primroses and starry white windflowers
Deep in the woods.

I remember the dogs, beloved friends.
Warm pink tongues and plumy tails,
Eager for games with sticks and stones,
Barking and leaping around our feet.
The feel of silky coats, darkened and wet
Beneath our childish, loving hands.

At the end of the day, in the long grey dusk,
The lift of the heart at the prospect of home.
Glowing peat fires in an oak-panelled room.
Oatcakes and honey. Hot buttered toast
And tayberry jam.
Treasures from a family long gone
But still alive in memory.

2017

SUNSET

They greeted me from their table in the window.
Bright in the rosy sunset glow.
Loving the world and everything in it.

We talked for a while,
Whilst we waited for a meal,
Of the beauty of the view
And this and that.
Old as they were their love was new.
The living proof that love can strike
At any age and any time.

I watched them as they ate.
Their hands reached out to touch and hold.
I heard their laughter and their joy.
Aware of each other. No one else.
But when they left
They touched my shoulder as they passed
Drawing me into their world.

I wished then you were there
To share in it.

2008

Village Fête

Their voices flow over me,
Like water over stones,
As I milk the cups and pour out the tea.
"Another slice of cake, Vicar?
My mother's recipe. A tried and tested favourite."
"How nice to see you, Mrs Smith.
So glad that you could make it."

The sun falls soft upon my back
In gentle water-colour light
But I am lost in a fiercer heat
Cutting its way through an indigo sky
To bleached, bare rock
Beside an azure sea.
I wonder where you are and what you do.
And whether you think of me as I do you.

Their voices come back to me
Like the buzzing of tetchy bees.
"We're running out of chocolate cake."
"I wish we'd brought more scones."
"Top up the urn, Evangeline."
"Oh dear, my feet are killing me."

But my ears are filled with the sound of bells.
The clamour of the city street.
The smell of cooking fills the air
Garlic and onions, peppers and fish.
My eyes see painted boats
Their high prows sharp against a blinding sky.
An iridescent sunset flames into a velvet night
Where the moon swings high amongst the lemon trees.

Their voices break through to me,
Noisy as birds in the chestnut trees.
"Thank God the weather held, my dear."
"We've taken more than last time."
"She's looking so much better."
"Well, now that's over for another year."

Firmly, I bolt the doors of memory,
Blending my voice with theirs,
Washing up cups and folding up trestles,
Boiling a kettle for our own cups of tea.

1980 / Revised 2015

TIME AND TIDE

In this close-companioned darkness
Let us forget that time and tide have not waited.
Let us disown, for a while, the aching limbs,
The wrinkles and unwanted flesh.
Let us pretend we are beginning.
That life, so full of promise, lies ahead.
But out on the shore the tide is racing
And in this room, the clock ticks on.

I shall lay my head upon your shoulder
As I did when we first met
And your arms will come around me
As they did when we were young.
Here, for a moment, time and tide are halted.

Together or apart
We are still one.

1990

Telephoning

When it comes to phoning you,
I try to ration myself.
Not more than once a week.
As, sadly, now that you are slowing down
Your time is precious with the big demands on you.

But there is one small blessing
In this nasty technical age.
The answer phone.
If you're not in,
I still can hear your voice.
That comforts me
And I can always ring again.

When you ring me
It is a celebration.
Christmas and Easter and Birthday
Rolled into one.
Knowing you've found the time
To ring me back.

2017

MIDSUMMER

Patterns of light on a worn, grey stair.
The coolness of stone at my feet.
Your smile in the shadows.
Your kiss at the door.
Love like a flame in the dark.

Remembering anew. Touching and giving,
Pierced by the light of your loving,
Wrapped in the silk of desire.
Diamond-sharp joy, twinned with despair.

Drowsy with heat in the shadowy darkness.
Holding you close with passion and longing.
Pushing aside the anguish of parting.
Smiling in moonlight.
Watching you smile.

1989

COMPENSATIONS

Yes, there are compensations
For catching the first bus
On a cold winter's day.
Waiting in the dark
With only a torch for company
To flag the bus down.

Then, as light grows,
Sitting alone on the 'bus
Listening to the silence,
Hoping the driver is awake,
I watch the mists rise across the meadows.
Ethereal, filled with magic,
Creating an enchanted place
Quite like no other.
This alone is compensation.

A little further on
The schoolkids clamber on,
Giggling and shouting,
Shattering my peace
But it doesn't really matter.
I have had my compensations.

2017

"Frauen Liebe und Leben"
(Robert Schumann)

This lovely cycle of songs
Written for Clara, his wife,
So rarely heard these days.
Not, perhaps, to modern taste.

I sang it in my youth.
Loved the music
But couldn't quite take on board
Old-fashioned German sentiments.
But sang it just the same
For the beauty of the songs.
Relying on musicality and voice.

They say of Shakespeare's Juliet
No actress should play the part
Until she's over forty.
By then she'll understand the role.
But sadly, then, she is too old
To look the part.

LOVING

And so it is for me but differently.
For now I have been there.
Sampled the wine. Bought the t-shirt.
I have known love and life and death.
I could sing them now
Better than before.

But the voice has gone.
It is too late.

2016

*Frauen Liebe and Lieben"
(A Woman's Love and Life)

TRAVELLER

He is lost in a forest of fear.
He cannot find the path.
Blunders on blindly in thickets of thorn,
Tearing his flesh on the briars,
Whilst skeleton trees twine their bones in his hair,
Trapping his feet in their tangle of roots.
Unspeakable things lie hidden on the forest floor
Waiting and watching, smelling his fear.

Then suddenly, the dark is lifted.
The pathway winds away beneath his feet.
Above the canopies of birdsong and of budding leaves,
The bony trees are fleshed with green.
The thicket blooms in springtide white.
Only the warm wind whispers
In the ferns and grasses of the forest floor.

His eyes upon the future, calm and bright,
Accepting what life may bring,
He will walk on
Towards the place of sun and clarity.
The summer fields beyond the trees.

2001

EMBERS

My mirror tells me I am growing old.
Best not to look.
Where did she go,
The girl I knew?

I grieve to see what time has done to you.
You, who were crystal-bright and clear.
Ardent and strong. Careless of life.
Illness and age have brought you low.
The winter dark draws near.
The ice-cold fear of losing you.

But, in your face your eyes are young
And in your arms I never think of death.
The numbing, winter cold is gone.
Past, present, future, now are one.
You are you, I am I.
Nothing has changed.

The fires have flamed and all but died,
Yet still the coals glow hotly red.
Stirred embers bring forth tongues of fire.
We may warm ourselves at the hearth
A little longer.

1992

MRS MUSSOLINI

The one that no one likes
And most try to avoid.
The Gorgon in the Surgery.
The Practice Nurse.

She makes my hackles rise.
Blood pressure soars.
And when she calls me to her room, she smiles
That patronising smile.
"And how are we today, my love?"
I can barely make reply.
I may be someone's love
But certainly not hers!

"Your pressure's up again," she says,
"How much, dear, do you drink?"
I, who imbibe in moderation,
Keep to a healthy diet,
Am tempted to say,
"Two bottles of gin a night
And, by the way, I smoke a pipe
And when I go out Clubbing
I always do the drugs."
But I keep my mouth shut tight.
She has no sense of humour.
I can't deny her nursing skills.

Efficient and sincere
But she knows it all, of course
And thinks that all of us
Are borderline dementia.
I know I should be tolerant
For I'm sure that she means well.
I only wish I didn't feel
Like beating out her brains.

Just keep her off my back!

2015

FAIRY TALES

Only in fairy tales does Cinderella find Prince Charming.
In reality, he's something far, far different.
If you kiss a frog he doesn't change.
He stays a frog.
Red Riding Hood, like Grandmamma, is eaten by the wolf.

Rubbing the genie's lamp brings nothing but smoke.
The Sleeping Beauty will sleep for ever
For no one will ever bother
To hack a way to her through the bramble wood.
Dick Whittington's cat turns out to be a tiger
And tears him to pieces.

And I, the song bird in a golden cage,
Beating my wings against the bars,
Will, no doubt, wait for ever
For someone to bring a key
To set me free.

I never learn.
I wait in hope for happy endings
To make the fairy tales come true.

2008

FLYING TO ARLANDA

The happiness begins the moment that I board the plane.
The babble of the Swedish voices all around.
This singing language I have learned to love.

The clouds are thick below
But there is sunshine in my heart.
Soon, very soon, I shall hear your voice,
Feel the warm clasp of your hand,
Your kiss of greeting.
The moment that the magic will begin.

We are coming in to land.
The dark clouds break.
Far as the eye can see
Are woods and fields and silvered lakes
Vibrant in the sun.
And far below the islands of an archipelago
Like shards of pottery
Floating on a sea of blue.
I stifle negative thought

That all too soon, within a day or two,
I shall be flying home again,
Straining to catch my last glimpse of the land below.

But does it feel like home?
Not anymore and never again.
For home to me is you.

2011

TIR NAN ÓG

Upon the shores of Lord Manannan's Isle
Do you wait for me, oh, *mo chridhe?*
My long lost love restored to me.
Beauteous and strong.
Fleet of foot and bright of eye
As I remember long ago.

Here amongst the *Daoine Sidhe*, the Shining Ones,
We will dwell together
On the island of eternal youth.
Eating the golden apples from the tree of life
Whilst the harp of the wind
Plays in the grasses of the shore
And the lark sings high above.

Hand in hand, we will walk together
Where the sapphire sea meets the white-gold sand.
Forever young, forever free
Upon the isle of *Tir Nan Ó'*

1992

"*Tir Nan Óg*" was the old pre-Christian Celtic idea of Heaven. Lord
*Manannan was the Lord of "Tir Nan Óg" and it was in his great white barge
that the spirits of the dead were conveyed there.*

"*The Daoine Sidhe*" *are the fairy people who dwelt in the hollow hills. The
Shining Ones, who maybe came to be the angels and saints after the coming of
Christianity.*

"*Mo chridhe*" *is translated as "my heart."*

JOHN MCNAB. SHEPHARD
(KILMORY, ARDNAMURCHAN)

They buried him here the way his forebears buried their dead,
In this ancient rough, round graveyard near the sea.
His face towards the islands of the West
And the fabled land of Tir Nan Og.
The place they believed was paradise.
Christian he was but the old ways linger on.

The seasons do not trouble him now.
The ice-cold winter winds across the land,
The ravening wind along the shore,
The awesome cauldron of the sea,
Boiling and seething in the bay.

The gentle breeze of summer suns
Will play above his worn old bones.
He will not know their heat.
Seamew and curlew will call to him in vain.
The summer flowers will bloom and fade
And if his sheep graze over him
They cannot break his sleep.
His life of toil is over.

No more for him the cruelty
And the crippling pains of age.
Sleep long and well,
Good John McNab.

1988

In memory of Mairhi McNab, his widow,
Whom I knew and loved.

STAR SONG

On a warm, moonless night we drove to the cliffs
Where the sea, unseen, sang soft below
And the south wind sighed around our nest.
Within the heaven of your arms, it seemed the stars swung low,
Scattering their glow-worm dust
Amongst the fennel and the flowering thyme.
"Listen," you said, "The stars are singing."
But the only music that I heard
Was the drumming of your heart
And the singing in my blood.

Under a chilly Suffolk sky, I stand alone
To watch the firework play of meteors,
Streaking across the vast high canopy of night.
Brilliant, remote and cold,
They keep their distance now
But, out of the past, I hear your voice
And the words you said, so long ago.

Above the silent clamour of the meteors
I hear, at last, the distant music of the spheres.
Piercingly sweet and crystal-clear,
The stars are singing.

1993

SPACE

Once upon a time I longed for space.
Craved it avidly, almost like a drug.
An escape from the hectic pace of life,
The pressure of work, the needs of those I loved.
I wanted nothing more than time to myself
To walk the hills and lie beside the sea.
Walking away the stress, sorting out my life.
Listening to the silence. Re-charging my batteries.

Now I have space, too much of it.
I am too old to walk the hills.
Alone in space, I sometimes feel
Adrift on some calm, flat sea,
Even between four walls.
Is it so strange to crave some life
Outside the emptiness?

What is it that they say?
"Be careful what you wish for.
You may be unlucky enough
To get it."

2017

TEARS

I carry within me a burden of tears;
The tears that form but never fall.
The unbearable weight of years
Of never showing what I feel.
Great frozen wastes of grief and loss
Too deep to ever melt in tears.

Yet still the frozen waters rise.
Build up as though against some mighty dam.
I live in fear that some day soon
The weight will make a breach in the wall
And as the dam comes trembling down
All the ice-melt will come pouring out.

Then will fall great rivers of tears.
Lakes, waterfalls and glacial streams,
Fountains, cascades and water spouts.
All the oceans of the world.
And I shall go on weeping
All the days of my life.

2011

IN THE SWISS ALPS

She dozes beside me on the coach
As we glide through deep, green valleys in the Alps,
Under the hanging woods and mighty mountain peaks.
A good and much loved friend
But she isn't *you.*

This is when I want you to be here
To share the beauty and the unexpected things.
You, too, would see the chapel hidden in the trees;
The last few swags of winter snow
Lingering in crevices between the slopes;
The big bells hanging from the necks of cows
In their lush green flowering alpine fields;
The over-dressed chalets with their waterfalls of flowers
And antique farmyard tools pinned hugger-mugger on their walls.
(Oh, how you would laugh at those.)

Now, when I see amongst the towering crags,
An eagle hover in a clear blue sky,
I want you here to see it all.
That's when I miss you most.

2016

NOBODY'S BUSINESS BUT MINE

I hear through the grapevine
That someone has said,
"How does she manage to travel so much?"

Are they reading my statements?
I'm angry.
It's none of their business
What I do with my life.

And just for the record.
I don't have a family.
Don't run a car
And don't keep a dog.
I save for my pleasures
And go where I please.

I know that they're envious
Of the pleasures I have
But *they* have the things
That I *never* have had.
No husband, no children.
Not even a dog.

What I do with my life is nobody's business.
Nobody's business but mine.

2017

WEIGHT OF WATER, BURDEN OF LAND

Over the telephone
You sound distressed, frustrated,
Almost desperate.
Feeling useless, with the weight of water
And the burden of land between us,
All I can say,
Over and over again, like a parrot,
Is, "I am so sorry."

But even if I were with you,
Face to face with your pain,
With the weight of water
And the burden of land behind me,
It would make no difference.
For you don't let anyone
Ever come too close.
Your pride would not allow.

So all I can say,
Over and over again, like a parrot,
Are the words that seem inadequate,
"I am so sorry."

2017

AFTERWARDS (FOR SILVIA WILLIAMS)

No one is left now to whom I can talk of you.
All now are gone who knew us as we were.
I can no longer bore my friends in praise of you,
Exchange remembrances, recall the laughter and the tears.

Although he never knew you,
My dog listens patiently,
Offering sympathy for a loss he never knew.
The birds know all about you
As do the sheep upon the hills
But they never make a comment
Or none I understand.

So, we walk the fells, the dog and I.
I tell our secrets to the earth.
To the shaft of sunlight on the mountain
And the morning mists upon the lake.
But nothing comes back to me.
Only the silence and an empty peace.

1991

ENGELBREKTKYRKAN

Even from the foot of the hill, on which it stands,
It is impressive.
Like some great mountain cliff.
Its lofty tower a lighthouse
Beaming light on a dark and troubled world.

Once through the outer doors, it isn't just impressive.
It is astonishing.
A place of majesty and awe.
This is a cavern in the hollow of a mountain.
So vast it almost overwhelms,
Seemingly hewn from solid rock.
Great ridged granite columns
Rise to reach so high a vault
It seems the vault must pierce the sky.

The pulpit is an eagle's nest perched on a mountain ledge.
The silver cover of the font set with precious stones.
Its treasures mined from depths below.
The great gold-gleaming hanging lamps
Are torches lightening up the mountain dark.

And there are far more subtle symbols here.
Powerful sculptures, awesome paintings, hidden carvings.
So much that one must seek and find.
Entities of doctrine and belief.
A history of salvation reaching back
Into the roots of Christian faith.

And there above the massive altar built of stone
Christ crucified looks down on us
With boundless love.
Whilst at his feet mankind looks up at Him
With praise and adoration.

I have found Him in many places
But here, in this place, cut down to insect size,
Dwarfed in the scheme of things,
I see the depth and strength of faith
And give thanks for His abiding love
And the wonders of Creation.

Here, I stand humbly in the presence of God
In the church at Englebrekt.

2010

This great church in the Jugendstil style of architecture was completed in 1912.

Solar Flower

Somebody said, "It's crap!"
I won't have that.
"No, no, it's not. It's KITSCH," I said,
"Something to raise a smile
On grey and dismal days."

A small, white daisy in a plastic pot,
A silly grin, a stem and two green leaves
That sway away the daylight hours
And sleep away the night.
But when the sun shines fully on
It just goes mad and rocks about,
Flapping its leaves like wings.

However low I feel, it makes me smile,
This silly, plastic toy.
Long, long ago I gave you one
Because like me,
You are a child inside.
Yours sits beside an orchid on a window sill.
Mine lives beside my kitchen sink
And helps me through the washing up.

Oh yes, it's KITSCH
But it is also FUN.

2012 / Revised 2017

BESIDE THE ROYAL CANAL

Under a grey September sky
We took a walk along the Royal Canal.
A time when autumn leaves began to change
From green to gold
And the last bright flowers of summer
Bravely displayed their colours to the sky.

Arm in arm, we slowly walked in step,
Flanked by our trusty walking sticks,
Stopping to rest, quite frequently,
On seats along the way.
A tourist boat came into sight.
"Just wait," I said, "someone will say,
"Look at that dear old couple walking there.
"How sweet they look" and then they'll wave.

And sure enough they did.
A line of hands along the boat
Began to wave at us.
Struggling to keep our balance, we waved back
And smiled in character.
Did what was expected of us.
And made some people laugh.

2017

SOUL

"Jag är stjärnan som speglar sig e dig.
Din skäll är mit hem. Jag har inget annat."

The words leap up at me
From off the printed page,
Blinding me with their dazzling truth and clarity.
It is exactly how I feel.

I have loved before and deeply
With body, mind and heart
But never like this.
There is a new dimension.
This time it is my soul that loves.
My soul has never loved before
And never will again.

The years close in
But the facets of love remain.
The body grows frail, the mind less keen.
The heart beats bravely on
But the soul glows bright in the gathering dark.
Reflecting itself in your distant star,
My soul flies home to you.

2014

The quotation in Swedish is from AFTONLAND by PAR LAGERKVIST
(Translated by W.H. AUDEN and LEIF SJÖBERG.)

"I am the star that mirrors itself in you.
Your soul is my home. I have no other."

SCHUCO BEAR

They found me in a junk shop
In the Netherlands,
Suspected my provenance
And took me back to England.
The man from Bonhams said,
"I think that he's a Schuco bear,
He could be worth a bit."

They put me in their shop
Amongst a hundred Teddy Bears
But they didn't sit me with the bright, posh bears,
(Swanky mohair, crisp faux fur)
Who turned their noses up at me.
I sat there all alone
Upon a dusty, wooden floor.
With my matted dirty fur,
Too old and poor to earn respect.

And then *she* came
She picked me up and cuddled me
And fell in love with me.
"I love his sad, sweet face," she said.
She paid my rather hefty price
And brought me home with her.

She gave me pride of place
Amongst her other toys
In the centre of a rocking chair
With bears and dogs and birds,
Some comic sheep, a velvet cat from Donegal,
A reindeer and two polar bears.
They have become my family.

They cluster up to me
And it doesn't matter that I am
No longer pristine white
For they respect my vast experience,
Seek my guidance and advice.
They've given me an honourable old age.

Sometimes when she isn't in
Or is fast asleep in bed,
They ask me for my fairy tales,
The ones learnt so long ago
When I was young and loved.
But I could tell them grimmer stories, too.

Dark memories of hardship and of war
Of death and of destruction,
Of persecution in an occupied land.
But I prefer to keep them to myself,
Some things best left alone.

I am a rescue bear.
I have survived
With all my limbs,
My eyes and ears.
I am a member of a proud bear heritage.

I am a Schuco Bear.

2017

BRIEF ENCOUNTER

Never very steady on my feet these days,
I teetered on the edge of a flight of steps.
No rail on which to place a hand.
A perilous uncertain place.

Then, at my side, appeared an arm,
A strong male arm
And someone said, "Can I assist?"

I could not turn to look,
Afraid that I could fall
But out of the corner of my eye
I caught a glimpse of a young blond Nordic god.
Danish or Swede, I think.

He helped me down the steps
And set me firmly on the cobblestones,
"As well you left the six-inch heels at home," he said.
I sighed, "I wore them once," I said,
"Long, long ago."

He laughed as he sped away to join his friends,
"Oh, not *that* long ago," he said.

Wow!

2016

WHAT REALLY MATTERS

It doesn't really matter
That you cannot feel for me
What I feel for you.
For you love me in your fashion,
My company and as a friend.
I am content with that.

What really matters is
The love I have for you.
You fill our days together
With laughter and delight.
You make my life worthwhile
And give me the reason to live.
I am content with that.

2017

CALYPSO'S ISLE

This is the isle where Ulysses, they say,
Was shipwrecked on its shores
And was bewitched by fair Calypso,
Who kept him captive in her cave for seven years,
Under the spell of beauty and the power of love.
I need no witch to hold me fast in thrall.
I am enchanted and seduced by the island itself.

I had forgotten just how beautiful it is
In warm, spring sun and cloudless skies.
The fields so full of flowers within the drystone walls.
Wild chrysanthemum and poppy,
Frail oxalis, pallid mallow,
The bright, pink spires of antirrhinum
And the giant gold heads of fennel
Growing like miniature forests in the rocks.
The fertile valleys, green with crops and vines.
Peach, fig and lemon trees
All shielded by high fences of bamboo.
The sound of the sea against the rocks
And sighing over stones.
I could stay longer than those seven years.
I could stay for ever.

What was it you said when we arrived,
Older and less mobile than before?
"We will achieve all that we can
And what we can't we'll dream about."
Well, we achieved it all
And visited the places that we love the most
But I am dreaming still
Of walking in the sun with you,
Listening to the sea
Sighing over stones.

2017

In the Lobby

I always try to get here early
So I can watch for you.
I see some guests arrive
Dragging their luggage up the steps.
Others check out.
Businessmen, friends meeting friends
Cluster about me,
Whilst I sit in my usual uncomfortable chair
Watching the street outside.

From here I see the buses come and go
And I wait for Number 55.
Almost on cue it comes.
I cannot see the middle doors from which you will alight
But I can tell, from the time it takes to close the doors,
That you, most likely, are on board
And when I see you slowly walk towards the crossing place
I watch you with a lightness of heart
And sadness, too.
For not so long ago I would see you stride across the road.
Now you walk slowly, needing your walking stick.

That's when I rise and go to stand
In front of that infernal automatic door
That closes when you reach the topmost step.
"Don't come up," I say, "I'm coming down."
Sparing you those stairs.

I see you smiling up at me
And life takes off again
Now you are here.

2017

STANDING HERE LOOKING BACK

I stand here looking back
At all the things that have happened in my life,
Even the things I would rather forget
And I am grateful that I still have memory.
I thank God for that.

Curiously in spite of everything,
I find I can still look forward to the future
With courage and with hope
And I thank God for that.

2016

ACKNOWLEDGEMENTS

My grateful thanks to Celia Rhys-Evans, Denise and Robert Vanston who printed the poems out for me and to Irene Beager who proof read them.